Self Care is NOT Selfish

A Busy Woman's Journey to Self-Care

Tasheka N. Cox Ed.D., LICSW

Copyright © 2019 Tasheka N. Cox
Layout and Design Copyright © 2019 Emerald Design Co.
All rights reservered.
ISBN-13: 978-1-69567-245-1

Table of Contents

Dedication	5
Self-Care is NOT Selfish: A Journey to Self-Discovery	6
Let's Talk About Stress	7
Self-Care	9
Section I: Self-Check	11
Section II: Six-Week Self-Care Journey	17
Pointers:	18
Week 1- Physical Self-Care	20
Week 2- Emotional Self-Care	22
Week 3- Mental Self-Care	24
Week 4- Spiritual Self-Care	26
Week 5- Social Self-Care	28
Week 6- Pleasure Self-Care	30
Section III: Self-Expression	32
Self-Care is NOT Selfish: Weekly Planner	42

Dedication

To my parents, thank you for all the sacrifices you made for me. You both left the only home you knew in Jamaica to bring my siblings and me to the US for a better chance at life. I don't have enough words to express my gratitude to you both.

To my husband, thank you for always being in my corner. Since the day I met you, you have encouraged me to reach my goals, dream big, and not let any obstacles get in my way. Your support, love, and encouragement are priceless to me.

To my children, Bryson, and Payten, you are the reasons I made self-care a priority in my life. I knew from the moment you stormed into my life that I had to be the best mommy I could be for you. You've both taught me, in your own ways, the importance of taking care of me. You showed me that a stressed mommy is not a happy mommy and because I want to try always to be the best mommy for you two, I will do whatever it takes to take care of me!

To my sister-friends, thank you all for always supporting me. We have spent countless hours laughing, crying, talking, and being there for each other. You have shown me that family doesn't always have to be blood. It can include those closest to you who capture your heart. Thanks for capturing my heart and allowing me to capture yours.

Self-Care is NOT Selfish:
A Journey to Self-Discovery

I wrote this book to help those of us who give so much to others give something back to ourselves. As moms, wives, daughters, career women, friends, and everything else between, we don't always leave space for our own needs because we get so busy tending to everyone else's needs. Our families, friends, and society expect so much from us, but what happens when we find ourselves not having much else to give because we've already given out so much?

I know the answer to this question because I have experienced firsthand the results of putting everyone else's needs in front of my own and getting caught up in the busyness of life. As a psychotherapist, a mom, a wife, a daughter, a sister, and a friend, I am always tending to someone else's needs. Don't get me wrong, I love all my roles, but sometimes they are exhausting, especially when I neglect my own needs in favor of taking care of those of others.

Many women whom I encounter in personal and professional contexts are willing to drop everything to help someone who calls on them for assistance. They will do that even if it means giving up time they had planned to spend doing something for themselves. Why is that? Do we get some badge of honor when we prioritize everyone else's needs before our own? Do we feel a sense of satisfaction when people compliment us for always being there for them? We bust our butts to make things happen for others and leave little time and energy to make something happen for ourselves.

Prioritizing time for ourselves may sound a bit counterintuitive because many of us have been raised to be nurturers, givers, go-getters, and selfless with our time. Listen, I was raised the same way, so I get it. But at what personal cost are we expending all our energy on everyone and everything around us? I know that all this is easier said than done, but at some point, we have to say enough is enough and realize that self-care is NOT selfish!

As a matter of fact, self-care is one of the most selfless things we can do for ourselves. Practicing self-care can be life-changing for women. We can't pour from empty cups. We can't give to others when we barely have enough to give to ourselves.

I created this workbook because I wanted women to take part in their own self-care journeys. The journey in this workbook is broken into three sections. Section One will allow you to notice where you are on your self-care journey by doing a short self-assessment. After discovering where you are, Section Two will allow you to embark on a six-week self-care journey. Section Three will help you express how you feel about where you are on your journey and determine what you can do to stay on your journey by integrating self-care into your life.

Before we get started, I want to congratulate you for permitting yourself to slow down and discover some great ways to take care of you!

Let's Talk About Stress

Before we begin our journey to self-care, we must first talk about why self-care is so important. Several years ago, I passed out at work and was rushed to the hospital. As that was happening, I remember saying to myself, "Lord, please let me be ok because I have so much stuff to do and I don't have time to be laid up in a hospital room." Can you believe that? There I was at work being carted off to the hospital on a stretcher, and all I could think about were the things I had on my To-Do list! Even in a crisis, I wasn't thinking about my own well-being. I couldn't even take care of myself, much less anything else at that point. Yet, I was worried about all I had to accomplish in the coming week.

I passed out because I had not been taking care of myself. I had not been taking care of myself because I was stressed and overwhelmed by my various commitments and responsibilities. According to the National Institute of Mental Health, stress is how our brain and body respond to the demands we place on them. Stress presents itself in many forms; not all stress is negative. In fact, some stress can motivate us to do things we need to do.

We all experience stress on some level throughout our lives, but when adverse or demanding circumstances put a strain on our mental, emotional, and physical health, we must pay attention to what is happening. I hadn't noticed the impact stress was having on my health. Indeed, it wasn't until I ended up in the hospital that I realized I was not dealing well with stress, and I needed help.

It is not enough, however, just to notice that we are stressed. Rather, we must actively reduce our stress. Long term stress or chronic stress can be very harmful to our bodies and can lead to serious health problems. Furthermore, long term stress can affect our mental health. It can increase anxiety and depression symptoms, for instance. The effects of stress can be long-lasting and persistent. According to the American Institute of Stress, common symptoms of stress include:

- Headaches
- Stomach pains
- Lack of energy
- Lack of focus
- Body pain
- Loss of interest in things you once enjoyed
- Overeating or under eating
- Forgetfulness
- Trouble sleeping
- Drug and alcohol misuse
- A decline in interest in sexual activity
- Anxiety/ Depression

Being overwhelmed and stressed landed me in the emergency room. It doesn't have to be the same for you if you pay attention to your symptoms and practice self-care to actively help reduce the stress that causes them. Anyone can feel stressed for any number of reasons. Common situations that can cause stress are:

- Money or financial problems
- Stressful job
- Child Rearing
- Parental care/family illness
- Relationship problems
- Health problems
- Not enough time to do things
- Not able to get a good sleep

Often, we overlook the situations that cause stress. Yet, stress can lead to elevated levels of cortisol (the stress hormone) which over time can cause serious damage to our system. Therefore, it is important to be aware of what's happening with us physically, emotionally, and mentally. Practicing self-care is a great way to notice and intentionally circumvent the negative effects of stress in our lives.

Self-Care

I begged the doctors to release me from the hospital the day I was admitted. They insisted that I needed to be monitored overnight. Nonetheless, I signed myself out of the hospital against medical advice. I can't believe I did that. Before I left, the doctor made me promise that I would follow up with my primary care doctor the following day. Although it took me several days to see my primary care doctor, I eventually did. The first thing she asked me was, "What have you been doing to take care of yourself?" I couldn't answer her question. All that came to mind were the things I did for others (my kids, my husband, my clients, my family, and my friends). I couldn't think of anything I was doing for myself. That realization stopped me in my tracks.

I decided that things were going to have to change. I decided to prioritize my own needs because I did not want to end up back in the emergency room. Since then, I have been committed to my own self-care. Although my journey has had its ups and downs, I have stayed the course, and I hope you can do the same.

Before we turn to your journey to self-care, let's talk about what self-care is. You may be thinking that practicing self-care is selfish and therefore believe that you don't have time to practice it. That's what I thought. I didn't see how I could take time out of my already jam-packed schedule to do something for myself. After all, I had kids to drop off and pick up from school, playdates and birthday parties to plan and attend, laundry to wash, fold, and put away, bills that needed to be paid, a house that needed to be cleaned, work that needed to be done, a husband to spend time with, friends who needed to talk with me, and myriad other things that chipped away at my time. Just thinking about my schedule used to make me anxious. It was too much; I was doing too much!

I realized, as I hope you will, too, that self-care is not a selfish act. On the contrary, self-care involves acts of kindness, love, and gratitude toward ourselves. Self-care also includes anything we do in the service of our mental, emotional, and physical health. Once I fully understood this, I no longer looked at self-care as being selfish. Rather, I saw it as something I needed to do for myself so that I could be the best me for myself and for those around me, especially those who I love and care about the most.

I found it fascinating how many ways there are to practice self-care. Through my self-care practice, I discovered the importance of silence, meditation, mindfulness, exercise, yoga, retreats, getaways, and so much more! I can't wait to see what you discover on your journey to self-care. As you embark upon this new way of being, I hope you find what you need to slow down the busyness and embrace the care that's needed for you to be the best you that you can be!

Section I: Self-Check

Stress can cause physical, emotional, and behavioral changes. Below are examples of some stress induced changes that I have experienced. Perhaps you have experienced some of these as well. If so, check the corresponding box.

Physical

Muscle aches	☐
Stomach pains	☐
Rapid heart beat	☐
Dizziness	☐
Tension headaches	☐
Blurred vision	☐
Shaky hands	☐
Other:	☐

Emotional

Depression	☐
Anxiety	☐
Panic	☐
Nervousness	☐
Restlessness	☐
Sadness	☐
Frustration	☐
Other:	☐

Behavioral

- [ ] Sleepiness
- [ ] Isolation
- [ ] Alchohol use
- [ ] Avoidance
- [ ] Impulsivity
- [ ] Hyperactivity
- [ ] Loss of Appetite
- [ ] Other:

Health Self-Check

This section is designed to identify areas of self-care in your life that are going well and those that may need a little more attention. Try not to judge yourself as you answer these questions. Take your time and be honest with your response.

Instructions: Circle the number that best describes your situation. At the end of each section, tally up your score and place the total on the line provided.

N= Never   **S= Sometimes**   **O= Often**   **A= Always**

Emotional Health

	N	S	O	A
1. I have a positive outlook on my life and future	1	2	3	4
2. I find joy in the things that I do in my life	1	2	3	4
3. I know that I have no control over others; I can only control myself	1	2	3	4
4. I practice gratitude for my life, family, and friends	1	2	3	4
5. I cope with life challenges in a healthy way	1	2	3	4

TOTAL: _____

Mental Health

	N	S	O	A
1. I recognize my symptoms when I feel stressed	1	2	3	4
2. I have healthy ways to relieve stress and don't need drinking to feel better after a hard day	1	2	3	4
3. I pursue interests and activities even when my energy is low	1	2	3	4
4. I recognize when I feel overwhelmed and need to take a break	1	2	3	4
5. I am up to the challenge of my daily life	1	2	3	4

TOTAL: _____

Physical Health

	N	S	O	A
1. I exercise several days a week for at least 30 minutes	1	2	3	4
2. I get 6 to 8 hours of sleep nightly	1	2	3	4
3. I eat a diet rich in nutrients	1	2	3	4
4. I drink at least 8 oz of water per day	1	2	3	4
5. I go to the doctor to get regular check-ups	1	2	3	4

TOTAL: _____

Spiritual Health

	N	S	O	A
1. I read for leisure/pleasure	1	2	3	4
2. I spend time in nature	1	2	3	4
3. I pray and/or meditate regularly	1	2	3	4
4. I work on forgiveness toward myself and others	1	2	3	4
5. I spend time reflecting on my life purpose	1	2	3	4

TOTAL: _____

Social Health

	N	S	O	A
1. I make time to hang out with friends	1	2	3	4
2. I have at least one close friend I can talk to	1	2	3	4
3. I am a member of a social organization	1	2	3	4
4. I volunteer my time to help others	1	2	3	4
5. I make time to try new experiences	1	2	3	4

TOTAL: _____

Pleasure Health

	N	S	O	A
1. I make time to have fun	1	2	3	4
2. I take vacations/staycations yearly	1	2	3	4
3. I intentionally go out to explore new places	1	2	3	4
4. I purposefully do activities that bring me joy	1	2	3	4
5. I enjoy my own company	1	2	3	4

TOTAL: _____

Personal Response

Now look at the areas where you have the highest scores and the lowest scores. Does anything surprise you? If so, what?

Would you like to improve your score in any area? If so, what area and why?

What do you think are the contributing factors to your scores in all areas?

Six Domains of Self-Care

Regardless of your response, you now have an opportunity to go on a six-week self-care journey. It will be a journey of discovery and awareness. This journey will guide you toward strategies for taking care of yourself how you want and when you want. The self-care journey is divided into the following six domains:

- Physical
- Emotional
- Mental
- Spiritual
- Social
- Pleasure

Focusing on these six domains will help you cultivate the deep awareness, compassion, and self-love that you need to care for every facet of yourself. Are you ready to go on this journey to self-care? Let's go!

Spiritual

Social

Mental

Pleasure

Emotional

Physical

Section II:
Six-Week Self-Care Journey

Taking a self-care journey can help you reduce or minimize your stress levels, improve your well-being, and help you maintain your health and wellness for years to come. When I first started on my self-care journey, I wasn't sure where to begin. I researched multiple self-care plans; I found some that worked better for me than others. I encourage you to do the same. Find an approach to self-care that will work with your life and your schedule.

The six-week journey is flexible enough for you to make it your own. You have several self-care activities from which to choose over a week. If you want to do more than one self-care activity per day, you can. Also, if you want to skip one day during a week, you can do that as well. I understand that life can get unpredictable for busy women. The point is to make self-care a priority by engaging in some of the self-care activities each week. Make a conscious effort to show yourself that self-care is NOT selfish!

No one can drink from an empty cup!

Pointers

One of the major obstacles that I faced when starting my self-care journey was time management.
At first, I found it hard to determine the best time of day to practice self-care. I decided to work backward on my calendar. I looked at all the things that were fixed on my calendar (i.e., work, kids' activities, homework, dinner, etc.). I discovered 30 minutes in the morning before everyone else woke up, free time during my lunch break at work, and a couple of hours after I put the kids down for bed at night. I decided to capitalize on those times, and so can you with the time you discover. Self-care activities don't have to last hours. You can do most activities in just a few minutes. We all get the same 24 hours per day, but it is up to us to decide how we are going to use them. Instead of giving all your time to others, why don't you devote some of it to your self-care? You can do it.

When starting a self-care journey, let the important people in your life (i.e., spouse, children, family members, friends) know your intentions.
That way, when you depart from your usual routine and take time out for yourself, they won't question it. Also, ask your people to serve as accountability partners and encouragers if you waver in your commitment to self-care. I am incredibly grateful for my husband, who reminds me to take my "me time" if I stray off course. He can tell when this happens because my mood tends to change. To get back on track, I take a break or practice my yoga and meditation.

Be gentle with yourself.
There will be days when you will not be able to get some of your self-care activities in because of whatever circumstances you're dealing with. If that happens, be compassionate with yourself. Allow yourself some space and resume your self-care activities immediately when you are able. Remember, it takes time to create new healthy habits. It won't happen overnight, just keep working towards your self-care goals in these areas.

Prioritize. Remember that self-care is NOT selfish.
When you prioritize your self-care, you put your needs on your list of important things to take care of. Throughout the day you may have many responsibilities which come with a to-do list, so make sure you put yourself on that to-do list. This strategy has been helpful for me when trying to find time for my self-care. In the morning, when I make my list of things to do for the day, I usually add one thing related to my self-care.

Try to designate a space in your home to practice home-based self-care. In my home, I created what I call my "Zen room," which is my kid and husband free zone when I am using it. In my Zen room, I have a yoga mat, a sitting area, a shaded lamp, some serene pictures on the wall, calming music, and aromatherapy. This is where I go to meditate, journal, pray, do yoga, and reflect. Try to claim a space in your home that is just for you!

Claim a space that is just for you!

Week 1:
Physical Self-Care

If you enjoy running a few miles a day outdoors or on the treadmill, then great; keep doing that. However, if you are like most people who try to fit in any type of exercise wherever and whenever you can, then you can do that during this week too! Physical self-care is not just about physically exerting yourself every day, but it also involves taking care of your physical body through a proper diet and exercise routine.

When I had the health scare that landed me in the emergency room, I'd not been taking care of my physical body. I had an underlying medical condition that I was not addressing because I was so busy with everything else. The condition that I have is easily managed, but it does require me to take a supplement regularly, schedule appointments with my doctor, eat balanced meals, and exercise. It can be challenging to do those things when I am feeling stressed, overwhelmed, and too busy to take care of my own needs.

My experience led me to focus on my personal self-care. I now enjoy physical activities that promote healthy self-care such as dancing, yoga, running, playing tennis, and being more conscious of what I eat. You too can discover physical activities that cultivate self-care. Try to find balance. It is important to stay active. Find something you enjoy and make sure you rest when you need to.

Here is a list of activities that you can do this week to practice physical self-care:

- Practice yoga and stretching.
- Go for a walk or run.
- Take a fitness class, dance, or workout at the gym.
- Get 6-8 hours of sleep.
- Schedule your annual physical check-ups and dental visits.
- Eat a healthy meal (make at least one of your meals during the day a healthy meal).
- Limit alcohol, caffeine, nicotine.
- Stay hydrated (drink at least eight-8 once glasses of water per day).
- If you're sick, stay home and rest.
- Take breaks when you need them throughout the day.
- Other: _____

Physical Self-Care Response

Were you able to try any of these activities this week or do something else for yourself physically?

If so, what were you able to do?

If not, what were some of the obstacles for you this week?

Is physical self-care something that you want to make a regular part of your self-care journey? If so, why?

If not, why not?

Week 2:
Emotional Self-Care

Emotional support is something we all need. Whether we are experiencing feelings of anger, frustration, or joy, it is important to understand why we are having these feelings. When we understand our feelings, then we are better equipped to accept or work through them.

Sharing our feelings and emotions with others can be hard at times. Although I encourage people all the time to let out what they have bottled up inside, I struggle with doing the same. Maybe it is because I am used to being the listener instead of the one who is listened to. Either way, I understand that it is healthy to practice emotional self-care and part of doing so is releasing in a healthy way our thoughts and feelings.

Holding everything inside and pretending I had it all together did nothing for me. In fact, it depleted me emotionally and physically. I found that practicing emotional self-care improved my emotional well-being. I hope that practicing some of the following activities will help you find the best way to improve your emotional well-being also.

Here is a list of activities you can choose from this week to practice emotional self-care:

- Accept your feelings. They are all ok.
- Write down your feelings on a notepad or journal.
- Cry when you need to.
- Show empathy to yourself and others.
- Laugh when you can.
- Practice mindfulness (be present to what you are feeling, thinking, and doing at the moment).
- Practice self-compassion.
- Take a break from social media.
- Talk to a counselor as needed.
- Communicate your thoughts and feelings clearly.
- Other: _____

Emotional Self-Care Response

Were you able to try any of these activities this week or do something else for yourself emotionally?

If so, what were you able to do?

If not, what were some of the obstacles for you this week?

Is emotional self-care something that you want to make a regular part of your self-care journey? Why or why not?

Week 3:
Mental Self-Care

When you are a busy working professional, stay at home parent, or caregiver, the daily responsibilities you carry can take a toll on you mentally. Mental fatigue can set in, which may make it challenging to remember what you need to get done. Practicing mental self-care can help you gain clarity and focus.

During the first five years of my children's lives, I felt like I was in a constant mental fog. I was trying to raise two young children, work full-time, be a wife, a friend, a daughter, a sister, and everything else. I experienced many mornings where I ran around the house like a madwoman looking for my keys only to discover that I left them in the door overnight. Once, I got home, went to sleep, and was woken up by neighbors knocking on my door at 1 a.m. because I hadn't closed my garage door when I got home. I was totally mentally exhausted most days. Sometimes I look back on those days and wonder how I made it.

When I realized that I could manage my exhaustion with some personal self-care, I started making changes in my life. I still experience mental fatigue from time to time, but now I practice moments of silence, mindfulness, and other mental activities to care for my mental well-being.

Here is a list of activities you can do this week that can help you practice mental self-care:

- Take action on something you've been avoiding
- Try a new activity
- Drive to a new place
- Make a bucket list
- Immerse yourself in a puzzle or brain game
- Read something you wouldn't normally study
- Listen to the sounds outside your window
- Listen to running water
- Practice mindful breathing
- Take moments of silence throughout your day
- Other: _____

Mental Self-Care Response

Were you able to try any of these activities this week or do something else for yourself mentally?

If so, what were you able to do?

If not, what were some of the obstacles for you this week?

Is mental self-care something that you want to make a regular part of your self-care journey? Why or why not?

Week 4:
Spiritual Self-Care

Spiritual self-care is how you nurture your connection with your higher power. Nurturing the connection helps us find meaning in our lives and recognize that something greater than us exists. It is important to cultivate care for both our physical body and our spiritual self. Awareness of our spiritual selves helps ground and center us, especially in stressful or troubling times.

The grace and mercies of my higher power were what enabled me to survive the early years as a newlywed, still in school, with two babies, and a full-time career. It was a lot, and I believe that I wouldn't have gotten through it if I had not done a lot of praying and meditating.

When I feel overwhelmed, as I often do, I read one of the inspirational quotes that I write in the notes section of my cell phone. I also often recite to myself, "worry about nothing; pray about everything." These little acts of self-care keep me grounded and centered. It is important to have something to keep you anchored when the waves of life come crashing as they often can.

Here is a list of activities that you can use to practice spiritual self-care:

- Read scripture or inspirational passage.
- Pray.
- Meditate.
- Read poetry.
- Write in your journal.
- Spend time in nature.
- Make a list of things you are grateful for.
- Work on forgiveness.
- Talk to a spiritual advisor.
- If you have a long-standing goal, look for ways to pursue it.
- Other: _____

Spiritual Self-Care Response

Were you able to try any of these activities this week or do something else for yourself spiritually?

If so, what were you able to do?

If not, what were some of the obstacles for you this week?

Is spiritual self-care something that you want to make a regular part of your self-care journey? Why or why not?

Week 5:
Social Self-Care

Another important aspect of self-care is our social being. We were not meant to live this life alone. As humans, we have a great capacity to relate to others. We tend to have a better quality of life when we have healthy interactions with others and the environment around us.

I moved away from my large family in Connecticut to pursue graduate school and my career in the Washington DC area several years ago. The plan was to return to my hometown, but then I met my wonderful husband, got married, and settled in the DC area. It wasn't until after we started having children that I realized how much I was missing my family of origin and the friends I grew up with. Luckily, I established some great new friendships with people who became like family to me.

I enjoy spending time with my friends and family, connecting, sharing, and socializing. Whether you are a social butterfly or a person who likes to keep to herself, I hope that you will use some of the following social self-care activities to take care of this part of your life.

Here is a list of activities you can practice this week for your social self-care:

- Go out to dinner with a good friend
- Call a friend on the phone to catch up
- Sign up for a book club, cooking class, etc.
- Join a support group or life group
- Play outside with your children and/or pets
- Volunteer at a soup kitchen, retirement home, youth center, etc.
- Enroll in a class to learn something new
- Hangout with friends after work
- Go out on dates with significant other, friend, or associate.
- Join a professional/ social networking group
- Other: _____

Social Self-Care Response

Were you able to try any of these activities this week or did you do something else for your social self-care?

If so, what were you able to do?

If not, what were some of the obstacles for you this week?

Is social self-care something that you want to make a regular part of your self-care journey? Why or why not?

Week 6: Pleasure Self-Care

Life is short. We spend much of our time so busy that, before we know it, months and years have passed. Sometimes we need to stop what we are doing and enjoy the simple pleasures of life. If we pay attention to what we are doing now, then we can find real pleasure in the day-to-day activities of our lives.

When I started practicing mindfulness, which is the practice of being attentive to, or present, at the moment, I realized that I had been missing out on many joyous moments in my daily life. I was a person who rushed through activities to get them done and say I did them. As a result, I missed out on the opportunity to enjoy participating in the activities. When I became mindful of what I was feeling, thinking, and doing, I noticed an abundance of pleasurable experiences in my life.

Now, when I take my kids to the park, I try not to multitask by checking my email or catching up on phone calls. Instead, I push them on the swing, and run, laugh, and giggle with them. I find such engagement with my kids to be much more pleasurable than checking emails while glancing up occasionally to make sure they are all right.

Whether I'm interacting with my family, my friends, or spending time alone, I experience pleasure from being fully present to whatever I am doing and whomever I am engaging with. I encourage you to be fully present this week as you engage in self-care activities that you enjoy.

Here are some activities that you can do this week, to help you with pleasure self-care:

- Take yourself out to eat.
- Be a tourist in your own city.
- Work in your garden or plant a flower.
- Watch a movie, listen to music, do artwork.
- Do something that makes you laugh.
- Do something adventurous.
- Take a vacation or have a staycation.
- Use aromatherapy or get a massage.
- Get a pedicure/manicure.
- Take a hot shower or a warm bath.
- Go outside, breathe in the fresh air, and feel the sun on your skin.
- Other: _____

Pleasure Self-Care Response

Were you able to try any of these activities this week or do something else for your own pleasure?

If so, what were you able to do?

If not, what were some of the obstacles for you this week?

Is pleasure self-care something that you want to make a regular part of your self-care journey? Why or why not?

Section III:
Self-Expression

You have dedicated the last six-weeks to taking care of you and learning that self-care is NOT selfish. I found it liberating to discover that through the practice of consistent self-care, I had the power to take care of my own personal well-being. It dawned on me that I could take time out for myself without feeling guilty. Taking time to care for my physical, mental, emotional, spiritual, social, and pleasurable self was what I needed to be a better person for myself and everyone else around me.

When we make a conscious effort to intentionally practice self-care, we may discover new things about ourselves. After this six-week journey, what did you discover about yourself and your need for self-care?

During your self-care journey, you may have experienced some obstacles or challenges. How were you able to get through those challenges? How will you continue to get through challenges as they arise?

Now that you have practiced self-care for the past six weeks and learned ways to alleviate some of the stress related to the challenges in your life, what do you think about self-care?

How do you feel about self-care?

What will you do now to make self-care a priority in your life?

Your Self-Care Plan

Since self-care is such a personal experience, I invite you to create your own self-care plan. You can use some of the activities suggested in the six-week journey, or you can come up with your own. Whichever you choose, make a plan that is personal to you! Your plan should not make you feel selfish, but rather it should serve as a reminder to dose yourself with self-love.

To that end, I'm providing a blank weekly planner. Feel free to make copies of the planner and keep using it for your self-care plans going forward.

I intentionally did not give you a lot of steps to follow to stay on your self-care journey because a journey is a journey. That is, any journey involves both successes and setbacks. You will likely experience highs and lows. I have tried plans to help me organize my schedule from hour to hour to fit in my self-care, but those didn't work for me. I grew frustrated and felt disappointed in myself when I did not stick to the hourly schedules. Instead, I relaxed and allowed my self-care to occur naturally every week. I listed it as a priority each week and then felt good about working it into my schedule. I encourage you to honor wherever you find yourself on your journey to self-care and do what works for you. It is important to remember that if you are mindful and intentional about your physical, emotional, mental, spiritual, social, and pleasurable health, you are practicing self-care. Remember, you don't need hours or a lot of money to practice self-care. In fact, it can be free. If you run out of ideas for self-care activities, refer to those that you used during the six-week journey and choose from among those. There are no rules about what you must do while practicing self-care. The only guideline is that you set time aside to focus on your well-being as opposed to that of others. Remember that self-care is NOT selfish!

Good luck on your journey.

You've got this!

I leave you with a list of what I wish for you:

I wish for you to have peace.

I wish for you to have joy in your heart.

I wish for you to feel loved.

I wish for you to experience calm.

I wish for you to have balance in your life.

I wish for you to always take care of you!

Self-Care is NOT Selfish Weekly Planner

Try to add one event to the calendar for each dimension of self-care. Use this planner as a reminder that you deserve self-care every day.

Month: _____   Monday's Date: _____

I am going to do these things to take care of myself in the following categories this week:

Physical

Emotional

Mental

Spiritual

Social

Pleasure

What worked?

What didn't work?

Monday

Tuesday

Wednesday

Thursday

Friday

Saturday

Sunday

Month: Monday's Date:

Monday

Tuesday

Wednesday

Thursday

Friday

Saturday

Sunday

I am going to do these things to take care of myself in the following categories this week:

Physical
Emotional
Mental
Spiritual
Social
Pleasure

What worked?

What didn't work?

Self-Care is NOT Selfish Weekly Planner

Try to add one event to the calendar for each dimension of self-care. Use this planner as a reminder that you deserve self-care every day.

Month: _____ Monday's Date: _____

I am going to do these things to take care of myself in the following categories this week:

Physical

Emotional

Mental

Spiritual

Social

Pleasure

What worked?

What didn't work?

Monday

Tuesday

Wednesday

Thursday

Friday

Saturday

Sunday

Month: _____ Monday's Date: _____

Monday

Tuesday

Wednesday

Thursday

Friday

Saturday

Sunday

I am going to do these things to take care of myself in the following categories this week:

Physical

Emotional

Mental

Spiritual

Social

Pleasure

What worked?

What didn't work?

Self-Care is NOT Selfish Weekly Planner

Try to add one event to the calendar for each dimension of self-care. Use this planner as a reminder that you deserve self-care every day.

Month: _____   Monday's Date: _____

I am going to do these things to take care of myself in the following categories this week:

Physical
Emotional
Mental
Spiritual
Social
Pleasure

Monday

Tuesday

Wednesday

Thursday

Friday

Saturday

Sunday

What worked?

What didn't work?

Month: _____   Monday's Date: _____

Monday

Tuesday

Wednesday

Thursday

Friday

Saturday

Sunday

I am going to do these things to take care of myself in the following categories this week:

Physical
Emotional
Mental
Spiritual
Social
Pleasure

What worked?

What didn't work?

Self-Care is NOT Selfish Weekly Planner

Try to add one event to the calendar for each dimension of self-care. Use this planner as a reminder that you deserve self-care every day.

Month: _____ **Monday's Date:** _____

I am going to do these things to take care of myself in the following categories this week:

- Physical
- Emotional
- Mental
- Spiritual
- Social
- Pleasure

What worked?

What didn't work?

Monday

Tuesday

Wednesday

Thursday

Friday

Saturday

Sunday

Month: Monday's Date:

Monday

Tuesday

Wednesday

Thursday

Friday

Saturday

Sunday

I am going to do these things to take care of myself in the following categories this week:

Physical

Emotional

Mental

Spiritual

Social

Pleasure

What worked?

What didn't work?

Self-Care is NOT Selfish Weekly Planner

Try to add one event to the calendar for each dimension of self-care. Use this planner as a reminder that you deserve self-care every day.

Month: _____   Monday's Date: _____

I am going to do these things to take care of myself in the following categories this week:

- Physical
- Emotional
- Mental
- Spiritual
- Social
- Pleasure

What worked?

What didn't work?

Monday

Tuesday

Wednesday

Thursday

Friday

Saturday

Sunday

Month: _____   Monday's Date: _____

Monday

Tuesday

Wednesday

Thursday

Friday

Saturday

Sunday

I am going to do these things to take care of myself in the following categories this week:

Physical
Emotional
Mental
Spiritual
Social
Pleasure

What worked?

What didn't work?

Self-Care is NOT Selfish Weekly Planner

Try to add one event to the calendar for each dimension of self-care. Use this planner as a reminder that you deserve self-care every day.

Month: _____   Monday's Date: _____

I am going to do these things to take care of myself in the following categories this week:

- Physical
- Emotional
- Mental
- Spiritual
- Social
- Pleasure

Monday

Tuesday

Wednesday

Thursday

Friday

Saturday

Sunday

What worked?

What didn't work?

Month: _____   Monday's Date: _____

Monday

Tuesday

Wednesday

Thursday

Friday

Saturday

Sunday

I am going to do these things to take care of myself in the following categories this week:

Physical
Emotional
Mental
Spiritual
Social
Pleasure

What worked?

What didn't work?

Self-Care is NOT Selfish Weekly Planner

Try to add one event to the calendar for each dimension of self-care. Use this planner as a reminder that you deserve self-care every day.

Month: _____ **Monday's Date:** _____

I am going to do these things to take care of myself in the following categories this week:

- Physical
- Emotional
- Mental
- Spiritual
- Social
- Pleasure

What worked?

What didn't work?

Monday

Tuesday

Wednesday

Thursday

Friday

Saturday

Sunday

Month: _____   Monday's Date: _____

Monday

Tuesday

Wednesday

Thursday

Friday

Saturday

Sunday

I am going to do these things to take care of myself in the following categories this week:

Physical
Emotional
Mental
Spiritual
Social
Pleasure

What worked?

What didn't work?

Self-Care is NOT Selfish Weekly Planner

Try to add one event to the calendar for each dimension of self-care. Use this planner as a reminder that you deserve self-care every day.

Month: _____   Monday's Date: _____

I am going to do these things to take care of myself in the following categories this week:

- Physical
- Emotional
- Mental
- Spiritual
- Social
- Pleasure

Monday

Tuesday

Wednesday

Thursday

Friday

Saturday

Sunday

What worked?

What didn't work?

About the Author

Tasheka N. Cox Ed.D., LICSW

Tasheka Cox is an experienced psychotherapist, mindfulness teacher, yoga instructor, speaker, and writer based in the Washington DC metropolitan area. Over the years, she has hosted self-care retreats, workshops, and seminars in different areas of the country. Her quest to help women slow down and make self-care a priority in their lives has inspired her to write this workbook.

Citation:

1. The American Institute of Stress (2019). https://www.stress.org/stress-effects.
2. The National Institute of Mental Health (2019. https://www.nami.org/Find-Support/Living-with-a-Mental-Health-Condition/Managing-Stress
3. How stress affects your health (2019). American Psychological Association. https://www.apa.org/helpcenter/stress.

Made in the USA
Monee, IL
09 January 2020